CHRISTIANITY AND ISLAM
BY
C.H. BECKER, PH.D.

PROFESSOR OF ORIENTAL HISTORY IN THE
COLONIAL INSTITUTE OF HAMBURG
TRANSLATED BY REV. H.J. CHAYTOR, M.A.
HEADMASTER OF PLYMOUTH COLLEGE

1909

TABLE OF CONTENTS

CHRISTIANITY AND ISLAM

A comparison of Christianity with
Muhammedanism or with any other religion must
be preceded by a statement of the objects with
which such comparison is undertaken, for the
possibilities which lie in this direction are
numerous. The missionary, for instance, may
consider that a knowledge of the similarities of
these religions would increase the efficacy of his
proselytising work: his purpose would thus be
wholly practical. The ecclesiastically minded
Christian, already convinced of the superiority of
his own religion, will be chiefly anxious to secure
scientific proof of the fact: the study of comparative
religion from this point of view was once a popular
branch of apologetics and is by no means out of
favour at the present day. Again, the inquirer whose
historical perspective is undisturbed by
ecclesiastical considerations, will approach the
subject with somewhat different interests. He will
expect the comparison to provide him with a clear
view of the influence which Christianity has exerted
upon other religions or has itself received from
them: or he may hope by comparing the general

development of special religious systems to gain a clearer insight into the growth of Christianity. Hence the object of such comparisons is to trace the course of analogous developments and the interaction of influence and so to increase the knowledge of religion in general or of our own religion in particular.

A world-religion, such as Christianity, is a highly complex structure and the evolution of such a system of belief is best understood by examining a religion to which we have not been bound by a thousand ties from the earliest days of our lives. If we take an alien religion as our subject of investigation, we shall not shrink from the consequences of the historical method: whereas, when we criticise Christianity, we are often unable to see the falsity of the pre-suppositions which we necessarily bring to the task of inquiry: our minds follow the doctrines of Christianity, even as our bodies perform their functions--in complete unconsciousness. At the same time we possess a very considerable knowledge of the development of Christianity, and this we owe largely to the help of analogy. Especially instructive is the comparison between Christianity and Buddhism. No less interesting are the discoveries to be attained by an inquiry into the development of Muhammedanism: here we can see the growth of tradition proceeding in the full light of historical criticism. We see the plain man, Muhammed, expressly declaring in the Qoran that he cannot perform miracles, yet gradually becoming a miracle worker and indeed the greatest of his class: he professes to be nothing more than a mortal man: he becomes the chief mediator between man and God. The scanty memorials of the man become voluminous biographies of the saint and increase from generation to generation.

Yet more remarkable is the fact that his utterances, his *logia*, if we may use the term, some few of which are certainly genuine, increase from year to year and form a large collection which is critically sifted and expounded. The aspirations of mankind attribute to him such words of the New Testament and of Greek philosophers as were especially popular or seemed worthy of Muhammed; the teaching also of the new ecclesiastical schools was invariably expressed in the form of proverbial utterances attributed to Muhammed, and these are now without exception regarded as authentic by the modern Moslem. In this way opinions often contradictory are covered by Muhummed's authority.

The traditions concerning Jesus offer an analogy. Our Gospels, for instance, relate the beautiful story of the plucking of the ears of corn on the Sabbath, with its famous moral application, "The Sabbath was made for man, and not man for the Sabbath." A Christian papyrus has been discovered which represents Jesus as explaining the sanctity of the Sabbath from the Judaeo-Christian point of view. "If ye keep not the Sabbath holy, ye shall not see the Father," is the statement in an uncanonical Gospel. In early Christian literature, contradictory sayings of Jesus are also to be found. Doubtless here, as in Muhammedan tradition, the problem originally was, what is to be my action in this or that question of practical life: answer is given in accordance with the religious attitude of the inquirer and Jesus and Muhammed are made to lend their authority to the teaching. Traditional literary form is then regarded as historical by later believers.

Examples of this kind might be multiplied, but enough has been said to show that much and, to some extent, new light may be thrown upon the development of Christian tradition, by an examination of Muhammedanism which rose from similar soil but a few centuries later, while its traditional developments have been much more completely preserved.

Such analogies as these can be found, however, in any of the world-religions, and we propose to devote our attention more particularly to the influences which Christianity and Islam exerted directly upon one another. While Muhammedanism has borrowed from its hereditary foe, it has also repaid part of the debt. By the very fact of its historical position Islam was at first indebted to Christianity; but in the department of Christian philosophy, it has also exerted its own influence. This influence cannot be compared with that of Greek or Jewish thought upon Christian speculation: Christian philosophy, as a metaphysical theory of existence, was however strongly influenced by Arabian thought before the outset of the Reformation. On the other hand the influence of Christianity upon Islam--and also upon Muhammed, though he owed more to Jewish thought--was so extensive that the coincidence of ideas upon the most important metaphysical questions is positively amazing.

There is a widespread belief even at the present day that Islam was a complete novelty and that the religion and culture of the Muhammedan world were wholly alien to Western medievalism. Such views are entirely false; during the Middle Ages Muhammedanism and Western culture were inspired by the same spirit. The fact has been obscured by the contrast between the two religions whose differences have been constantly exaggerated and by dissimilarities of language and nationality. To retrace in full detail the close connection which unites Christianity and Islam would be the work of years. Within the scope of the present volume, all that can be done is to explain the points of contact between Christian and Muhammedan theories of life and religion. Such is the object of the following pages. We shall first treat of Muhammed personally, because his rise as a religious force will explain the possibility of later developments.

This statement also explains the sense in which we shall use the term Christianity. Muhammedanism has no connection with post-Reformation Christianity and meets it only in the mission field. Practical questions there arise which lie beyond the limits of our subject, as we have already indicated. Our interests are concerned with the mediaeval Church, when Christianity first imposed its ideas upon Muhammedanism at the time of its rise in the East, and afterwards received a material extension of its own horizon through the rapid progress of its protégé. Our task is to analyse and explain these special relations between the two systems of thought.

The religion now known as Islam is as near to the preaching of Muhammed or as remote from it, as modern Catholicism or Protestant Christianity is at variance or in harmony with the teaching of Jesus. The simple beliefs of the prophet and his contemporaries are separated by a long course of development from the complicated religious system in its unity and diversity which Islam now presents to us. The course of this development was greatly influenced by Christianity, but Christian ideas had been operative upon Muhammed's eager intellectual life at an even earlier date. We must attempt to realise the working of his mind, if we are to gain a comprehension of the original position of Islam with regard to Christianity. The task is not so difficult in Muhammed's case as in that of others who have founded religious systems: we have records of his philosophical views, important even though fragmentary, while vivid descriptions of his experiences have been transmitted to us in his own words, which have escaped the modifying influence of tradition at second hand. Muhammed had an indefinite idea of the word of God as known to him from other religions. He was unable to realise this idea effectively except as an immediate revelation; hence throughout the Qoran he represents God as speaking in the first person and himself appears as the interlocutor. Even direct commands to the congregation are introduced by the stereotyped "speak"; it was of primary importance that the Qoran should be regarded as God's word and not as man's. This fact largely contributed to secure an uncontaminated transmission of the text, which seems also to have been left by Muhammed himself in definite form. Its intentional obscurity of expression does not facilitate the task of the inquirer, but it provides, none the less, considerable information concerning the religious progress of its author. Here we are upon firmer ground than when we attempt to describe Muhammed's outward life, the first half of which is wrapped in obscurity no less profound than that which veils the youth of the Founder of Christianity.

Muhammed's contemporaries lived amid religious indifference. The majority of the Arabs were heathen and their religious aspirations were satisfied by local cults of the Old Semitic character. They may have preserved the religious institutions of the great South Arabian civilisation, which was then in a state of decadence; the beginnings of Islam may also have been influenced by the ideas of this civilisation, which research is only now revealing to us: but these points must remain undecided for the time being. South Arabian civilisation was certainly not confined to the South, nor could an organised township such as Mecca remain outside its sphere of influence: but the scanty information which has reached us concerning the religious life of the Arabs anterior to Islam might also be explained by supposing them to have followed a similar course of development. In any case, it is advisable to reserve judgment until documentary proof can replace ingenious conjecture. The difficulty of the problem is increased by the fact that Jewish and especially Christian ideas penetrated from the South and that their influence cannot be estimated. The important point for us to consider is the existence of Christianity in Southern Arabia before the Muhammedan period. Nor was the South its only starting-point: Christian doctrine came to Arabia from the North, from Syria and Babylonia, and numerous conversions, for the most part of whole tribes, were made. On the frontiers also Arabian merchants came into continual contact with Christianity and foreign merchants of the Christian

faith could be found throughout Arabia. But for the
Arabian migration and the simultaneous foundation
of a new Arabian religion, there is no doubt that the
whole peninsula would have been speedily
converted to Christianity.

The chief rival of Christianity was Judaism, which
was represented in Northern as in Southern Arabia
by strong colonies of Jews, who made proselytes,
although their strict ritualism was uncongenial to
the Arab temperament which preferred conversion
to Christianity (naturally only as a matter of form).
In addition to Jewish, Christian, and Old Semitic
influences, Zoroastrian ideas and customs were also
known in Arabia, as is likely enough in view of the
proximity of the Persian empire.

These various elements aroused in Muhammed's
mind a vague idea of religion. His experience was
that of the eighteenth-century theologians who
suddenly observed that Christianity was but one of
many very similar and intelligible religions, and
thus inevitably conceived the idea of a pure and
natural religious system fundamental to all others.
Judaism and Christianity were the only religions
which forced themselves upon Muhammed's
consciousness and with the general characteristics
of which he was acquainted. He never read any part
of the Old or New Testament: his references to
Christianity show that his knowledge of the Bible
was derived from hearsay and that his informants
were not representative of the great religious sects:
Muhammed's account of Jesus and His work, as
given in the Qoran, is based upon the apocryphal
accretions which grew round the Christian doctrine.
When Muhammed proceeded to compare the great
religions of the Old and New Testaments with the

superficial pietism of his own compatriots, he was especially impressed with the seriousness of the Hebrews and Christians which contrasted strongly with the indifference of the heathen Arabs. The Arab was familiar with the conception of an almighty God, and this idea had not been obscured by the worship of trees, stones, fire and the heavenly bodies: but his reverence for this God was somewhat impersonal and he felt no instinct to approach Him, unless he had some hopes or fears to satisfy. The idea of a reckoning between man and God was alien to the Arab mind. Christian and Jewish influence became operative upon Muhammed with reference to this special point. The idea of the day of judgment, when an account of earthly deeds and misdeeds will be required, when the joys of Paradise will be opened to the good and the bad will be cast into the fiery abyss, such was the great idea, which suddenly filled Muhammed's mind and dispelled the indifference begotten of routine and stirred his mental powers.

Polytheism was incompatible with the idea of God as a judge supreme and righteous, but yet merciful. Thus monotheism was indissolubly connected with Muhammed's first religious impulses, though the dogma had not assumed the polemical form in which it afterwards confronted the old Arabian and Christian beliefs. But a mind stirred by religious emotion only rose to the height of prophetic power after a long course of development which human knowledge can but dimly surmise. Christianity and Judaism had their sacred books which the founders of these religions had produced. In them were the words of God, transmitted through Moses to the Jews and through Jesus to the Christians. Jesus and

Moses had been God's ambassadors to their peoples. Who then could bring to the Arabs the glad tidings which should guide them to the happy fields of Paradise? Among primitive peoples God is regarded as very near to man. The Arabs had, their fortune-tellers and augurs who cast lots before God and explained His will in mysterious rhythmical utterances. Muhammed was at first more intimately connected with this class of Arab fortune-tellers than is usually supposed. The best proof of the fact is the vehemence with which he repudiates all comparison between these fortune-tellers and himself, even as early Christian apologetics and polemics attacked the rival cults of the later classical world, which possessed forms of ritual akin to those observed by Christianity. The existence of a fortune-telling class among the Arabs shows that Muhammed may well have been endowed with psychological tendencies which only awaited the vivifying influence of Judaism and Christianity to emerge as the prophetic impulse forcing him to stand forth in public and to stir the people from their indifference: "Be ye converted, for the day of judgment is at hand: God has declared it unto me, as he declared it unto Moses and Jesus. I am the apostle of God to you, Arabs. Salvation is yours only if ye submit to the will of God preached by me." This act of submission Muhammed calls Islam. Thus at the hour of Islam's birth, before its founder had proclaimed his ideas, the influence of Christianity is indisputable. It was this influence which made of the Arab seer and inspired prophet, the apostle of God.

Muhammed regarded Judaism and Christianity as religious movements purely national in character.

God in His mercy had announced His will to different nations through His prophets. As God's word had been interpreted for the Jews and for the Christians, so there was to be a special interpretation for the benefit of the Arabs. These interpretations were naturally identical in manner and differed only as regards place and time. Muhammed had heard of the Jewish Messiah and of the Christian Paraclete, whom, however, he failed to identify with the Holy Ghost and he applied to himself the allusions to one who should come after Moses and Jesus. Thus in the Qoran 61.6 we read, "Jesus, the Son of Mary, said: Children of Israel, I am God's apostle to you. I confirm in your hands the Thora (the law) and I announce the coming of another apostle after me whose name is Ahmed." Ahmed is the equivalent of Muhammed. The verse has been variously interpreted and even rejected as an interpolation: but its authenticity is attested by its perfect correspondence with what we know of Muhammed's pretensions.

To trace in detail the development of his attitude towards Christianity is a more difficult task than to discover the growth of his views upon Judaism; probably he pursued a similar course in either case. At first he assumed the identity of the two religions with one another and with his own doctrine; afterwards he regarded them as advancing by gradations. Adam, Abraham, Moses, Jesus, and Muhammed, these in his opinion were the chief stages in the divine scheme of salvation. Each was respectively confirmed or abolished by the revelation which followed it, nor is this theory of Muhammed's shaken by the fact that each revelation was given to a different nation. He regards all preceding prophets in the light of his own personality. They were all sent to people who refused them a hearing at the moment. Punishment follows and the prophet finds a body of believers elsewhere. These temporary punishments are confused with the final Judgment; in fact Muhammed's system was not clearly thought out. The several prophets were but men, whose earthly careers were necessarily crowned with triumph: hence the crucifixion of Jesus is a malicious invention of the Jews, who in reality crucified some other sufferer, while Jesus entered the divine glory. Thus Muhammed has no idea of the importance of the Crucifixion to the Christian Church, as is shown by his treatment of it as a Jewish falsehood. In fact, he develops the habit of characterising as false any statement in contradiction with his ideas, and this tendency is especially obvious in his dealings with Judaism, of which he gained a more intimate knowledge. At first he would refer sceptics to Christian and Jewish doctrine for confirmation of his own teaching. The fact that with no knowledge of the Old or New Testament, he had proclaimed doctrines materially similar and the fact that these Scriptures referred to himself, were proofs of his inspired power, let doubters say what they would. A closer acquaintance with these Scriptures showed him that the divergencies which he stigmatised as falsifications denoted in reality vast doctrinal differences.

In order to understand Muhammed's attitude towards Christianity, we will examine in greater detail his view of this religion, the portions of it which he accepted or which he rejected as unauthentic. In the first place he must have regarded the Trinity as repugnant to reason: he considered the Christian Trinity as consisting of God the Father, Mary the Mother of God, and Jesus the Son of God. In the Qoran, God says, "Hast thou, Jesus, said to men, Regard me and my mother as Gods by the side of God?" Jesus replies, "I will say nothing but the truth. I have but preached, Pray to God, who is my Lord and your Lord" (5.116, f). Hence it has been inferred that Muhammed's knowledge of Christianity was derived from some particular Christian sect, such as the Tritheists or the Arab female sect of the Collyridians who worshipped the Virgin Mary with exaggerated reverence and assigned divine honours to her. It is also possible that we have here a development of some Gnostic conception which regarded the Holy Ghost as of feminine gender, as Semites would do;[A] instances of this change are to be found in the well-known Hymn of the Soul in the Acts of Thomas, in the Gospel to the Egyptians and elsewhere. I am inclined, however, to think it more probable that Muhammed had heard of Mariolatry and of the "mother of God," a title which then was a highly popular catchword, and that the apotheosis of Jesus was known to him and also the doctrine of the Trinity by name. Further than this his knowledge did not extend; although he knows the Holy Ghost and identifies him with Jesus, none the less his primitive reasoning, under the influence of many old beliefs, explained the mysterious triad of the Trinity as husband, wife, and son. This fact is enough to prove that his theory of Christianity was formed by combining isolated scraps of information and that he cannot have had any direct instruction from a Christian knowing the outlines of his faith.

[Footnote A: The word for "Spirit" is of the feminine gender in the Semitic languages.] Muhammed must also have denied the divinity of Christ: this is an obvious result of the course of mental development which we have described and of his characteristically Semitic theory of the nature of God. To him, God is one, never begetting and never begotten. Denying the divinity of Jesus, Muhammed naturally denies the redemption through the Cross and also the fact of the Crucifixion. Yet, strangely enough he accepted the miraculous birth; nor did he hesitate to provide this purely human Jesus with all miraculous attributes; these were a proof of his divine commission, and marvellous details of this nature aroused the interest of his hearers.

Mary the sister of Ahron--an obvious confusion with the Old Testament Miriam--had been devoted to the service of God by her mother's vow, and lives in the temple under the guardianship of Zacharias, to whom a later heir is born in answer to his prayers, namely John, the forerunner of the Holy Ghost. The birth is announced to Mary and she brings forth Jesus under a palm-tree, near which is a running spring and by the dates of which she is fed. On her return home she is received with reproaches by her family but merely points in reply to the new-born babe, who suddenly speaks from his cradle, asserting that he is the prophet of God. Afterwards Jesus performs all kinds of miracles, forms birds out of clay and makes them fly, heals the blind and lepers, raises the dead, etc., and even brings down from heaven a table ready spread. The Jews will not believe him, but the youth follow him. He is not killed, but translated to God. Christians are not agreed upon the manner of his death and the Jews have invented the story of the Crucifixion. Muhammed's knowledge of Christianity thus consists of certain isolated details, partly apocryphal, partly canonical, together with a hazy idea of the fundamental dogmas. Thus the influence of Christianity upon him was entirely indirect. The Muhammedan movement at its outset was influenced not by the real Christianity of the time but by a Christianity which Muhammed criticised in certain details and forced into harmony with his preconceived ideas. His imagination was profoundly impressed by the existence of Christianity as a revealed religion with a founder of its own. Certain features of Christianity and of Judaism, prayer, purification, solemn festivals, scriptures, prophets and so forth were regarded by him as essential to any religious community, because they happened to belong both to Judaism and to Christianity. He therefore adopted or wished to adopt these institutions.

During the period of his life at Medina, Muhammed abandoned his original idea of preaching the doctrines which Moses and Jesus had proclaimed. This new development was the outcome of a struggle with Judaism following upon an unsuccessful attempt at compromise. In point of fact Judaism and Christianity were as widely different from one another as they were from his own teaching and he was more than ever inclined to regard as his special forerunner, Abraham, who had preceded both Moses and Jesus, and was revered by both religions as the man of God. He then brought Abraham into connection with the ancient Meccan Ka'ba worship: the Ka'ba or die was a sacred stone edifice, in one corner of which the "black stone" had been built in: this stone was an object of reverence to the ancient Arabs, as it still is to the Muhammedans. Thus Islam gradually assumed the form of an Arab religion, developing universalist tendencies in the ultimate course of events. Muhammed, therefore, as he was the last in the ranks of the prophets, must also be the greatest. He epitomised all prophecy and Islam superseded every revealed religion of earlier date.

Muhammed's original view that earlier religions had been founded by God's will and through divine revelation, led both him and his successors to make an important concession: adherents of other religions were not compelled to adopt Islam. They were allowed to observe their own faith unhindered, if they surrendered without fighting, and were even protected against their enemies, in return for which they had to pay tribute to their Muslim masters; this was levied as a kind of poll-tax. Thus we read in the Qoran (ix. 29) that "those who possess Scriptures," i.e. the Jews and Christians, who did not accept Islam were to be attacked until they paid the *gizja* or tribute. Thus the object of a religious war upon the Christians is not expressed by the cry "Death or Islam"; such attacks were intended merely to extort an acknowledgment of Muhammedan supremacy, not to abolish freedom of religious observance. It would be incorrect for the most part to regard the warrior bands which started from Arabia as inspired by religious enthusiasm or to attribute to them the fanaticism which was first aroused by the crusades and in an even greater degree by the later Turkish wars. The Muhammedan fanatics of the wars of conquest, whose reputation was famous among later generations, felt but a very scanty interest in religion and occasionally displayed an ignorance of its fundamental tenets which we can hardly exaggerate. The fact is fully consistent with the impulses to which the Arab migrations were due. These impulses were economic and the new religion was nothing more than a party cry of unifying power, though there is no reason to suppose that it was not a real moral force in the life of Muhammed and his immediate contemporaries.

Anti-Christian fanaticism there was therefore none. Even in early years Muhammedans never refused to worship in the same buildings as Christians. The various insulting regulations which tradition represents Christians as forced to endure were directed not so much against the adherents of another faith as against the barely tolerated inhabitants of a subjugated state. It is true that the distinction is often difficult to observe, as religion and nationality were one and the same thing to Muhammedans. In any case religious animosity was a very subordinate phenomenon. It was a gradual development and seems to me to have made a spasmodic beginning in the first century under the influence of ideas adopted from Christianity. It may seem paradoxical to assert that it was Christian influence which first stirred Islam to religious animosity and armed it with the sword against Christianity, but the hypothesis becomes highly probable when we have realised the indifferentism of the Muhammedan conquerors.

We shall constantly see hereafter how much they owed in every department of intellectual life to the teaching of the races which they subjugated. Their attitude towards other beliefs was never so intolerant as was that of Christendom at that period. Christianity may well have been the teaching influence in this department of life as in others. Moreover at all times and especially in the first century the position of Christians has been very tolerable, even though the Muslims regarded them as an inferior class, Christians were able to rise to the highest offices of state, even to the post of vizier, without any compulsion to renounce their faith. Even during the period of the crusades when the religious opposition was greatly intensified, again through Christian policy, Christian officials cannot have been uncommon: otherwise Muslim theorists would never have uttered their constant invectives against the employment of Christians in administrative duties. Naturally zealots appeared at all times on the Muhammedan as well as on the Christian side and occasionally isolated acts of oppression took place: these were, however, exceptional. So late as the eleventh century, church funeral processions were able to pass through the streets of Bagdad with all the emblems of Christianity and disturbances were recorded by the chroniclers as exceptional. In Egypt, Christian festivals were also regarded to some extent as holidays by the Muhammedan population. We have but to imagine these conditions reversed in a Christian kingdom of the early middle ages and the probability of my theory will become obvious. The Christians of the East, who had broken for the most part with the orthodox Church, also regarded Islam as a lesser evil than the Byzantine established Church. Moreover Islam, as being both a political and ecclesiastical organisation, regarded the Christian church as a state within a state and

permitted it to preserve its own juridical and at first
its own governmental rights. Application was made
to the bishops when anything was required from the
community and the churches were used as taxation
offices. This was all in the interests of the clergy
who thus found their traditional claims realised.
These relations were naturally modified in the
course of centuries; the crusades, the Turkish wars
and the great expansion of Europe widened the
breach between Christianity and Islam, while as the
East was gradually brought under ecclesiastical
influence, the contrast grew deeper: the theory,
however, that the Muhammedan conquerors and
their successors were inspired by a fanatical hatred
of Christianity is a fiction invented by Christians.
We have now to examine this early development of
Islam in somewhat greater detail: indeed, to secure
a more general appreciation of this point is the
object of the present work.

The relationship of the Qoran to Christianity has
been already noted: it was a book which preached
rather than taught and enounced isolated laws but
no connected system. Islam was a clear and simple
war-cry betokening merely a recognition of Arab
supremacy, of the unity of God and of Muhammed's
prophetic mission. But in a few centuries Islam
became a complex religious structure, a confusion
of Greek philosophy and Roman law, accurately
regulating every department of human life from the
deepest problems of morality to the daily use of the
toothpick, and the fashions of dress and hair. This
change from the simplicity of the founder's religious
teaching to a system of practical morality often
wholly divergent from primitive doctrine, is a
transformation which all the great religions of the

world have undergone. Religious founders have succeeded in rousing the sense of true religion in the human heart. Religious systems result from the interaction of this impulse with pre-existing capacities for civilisation. The highest attainments of human life are dependent upon circumstances of time and place, and environment often exerts a more powerful influence than creative power. The teaching of Jesus was almost overpowered by the Graeco-Oriental culture of later Hellenism. Dissensions persist even now because millions of people are unable to distinguish pure religion from the forms of expression belonging to an extinct civilisation. Islam went through a similar course of development and assumed the spiritual panoply which was ready to hand. Here, as elsewhere, this defence was a necessity during the period of struggle, but became a crushing burden during the peace which followed victory, for the reason that it was regarded as inseparable from the wearer of it. From this point of view the analogy with Christianity will appear extremely striking, but it is something more than an analogy: the Oriental Hellenism of antiquity was to Christianity that which the Christian Oriental Hellenism of a few centuries later was to Islam.

We must now attempt to realise the nature of this event so important in the history of the world. A nomadic people, recently united, not devoid of culture, but with a very limited range of ideas, suddenly gains supremacy over a wide and populous district with an ancient civilisation. These nomads are as yet hardly conscious of their political unity and the individualism of the several tribes composing it is still a disruptive force: yet they can secure domination over countries such as Egypt and Babylonia, with complex constitutional systems, where climatic conditions, the nature of the soil and centuries of work have combined to develop an intricate administrative system, which newcomers could not be expected to understand, much less to recreate or to remodel. Yet the theory has long been held that the Arabs entirely reorganised the constitutions of these countries. Excessive importance has been attached to the statements of Arab authors, who naturally regarded Islam as the beginning of all things. In every detail of practical life they regarded the prophet and his contemporaries as their ruling ideal, and therefore naturally assumed that the constitutional practices of the prophet were his own invention. The organisation of the conquering race with its tribal subordination was certainly purely Arab in origin. In fact the conquerors seemed so unable to adapt themselves to the conditions with which they met, that foreigners who joined their ranks were admitted to the Muhammedan confederacy only as clients of the various Arab tribes. This was, however, a mere question of outward form: the internal organisation continued unchanged, as it was bound to continue unless chaos were to be the consequence. In fact, pre-existing administrative regulations were so far retained that the old customs duties on the former frontiers were levied as before, though they represented an institution wholly alien to the spirit of the Muhammedan empire. Those Muhammedan authors, who describe the administrative organisation, recognise only the taxes which Islam regarded as lawful and characterise others as malpractices which had crept in at a later date. It is remarkable that these so-called subsequent malpractices correspond with Byzantine and Persian usage before the conquest: but tradition will not admit the fact that these remained unchanged. The same fact is obvious when we consider the progress of civilisation in general. In every case the Arabs merely develop the social and economic achievements of the conquered races to further issues. Such progress could indeed only be modified by a general upheaval of existing conditions and no such movement ever took place. The Germanic tribes destroyed the civilisations with which they met; they adopted many of the institutions of Christian antiquity, but found them an impediment to the development of their own genius. The Arabs simply continued to develop the civilisation of post-classical antiquity, with which they had come in contact.

This procedure may seem entirely natural in the department of economic life, but by no means inevitable where intellectual progress is concerned. Yet a similar course was followed in either case, as may be proved by dispassionate examination. Islam was a rising force, a faith rather of experience than of theory or dogma, when it raised its claims against Christianity, which represented all pre-existing intellectual culture. A settlement of these claims was necessary and the military triumphs are but the prelude to a great accommodation of intellectual interests. In this Christianity played the chief part, though Judaism is also represented: I am inclined, however, to think that Jewish ideas as they are expressed in the Qoran were often transmitted through the medium of Christianity. There is no doubt that in Medina Muhammed was under direct

Jewish influence of extraordinary power. Even at
that time Jewish ideas may have been in circulation,
not only in the Qoran but also in oral tradition,
which afterwards became stereotyped: at the same
time Muhammed's utterances against the Jews
eventually became so strong during the Medina
period, for political reasons, that I can hardly
imagine the traditions in their final form to have
been adopted directly from the Jews. The case of
Jewish converts is a different matter. But in
Christianity also much Jewish wisdom was to be
found at that time and it is well known that even the
Eastern churches regarded numerous precepts of the
Old Testament, including those that dealt with
ritual, as binding upon them. In any case the spirit
of Judaism is present, either directly or working
through Christianity, as an influence wherever
Islam accommodated itself to the new intellectual
and spiritual life which it had encountered. It was a
compromise which affected the most trivial details
of life, and in these matters religious scrupulosity
was carried to a ridiculous point: here we may see
the outcome of that Judaism which, as has been
said, was then a definite element in Eastern
Christianity. Together with Jewish, Greek and
classical ideas were also naturally operative, while
Persian and other ancient Oriental conceptions were
transmitted to Islam by Christianity: these instances
I have collectively termed Christian because
Christianity then represented the whole of later
classical intellectualism, which influenced Islam for
the most part through Christianity.

It seems that the communication of these ideas to
Muhammedanism was impeded by the necessity of
translating them not only into a kindred language,

but into one of wholly different linguistic structure. For Muhammedanism the difficulty was lessened by the fact that it had learned Christianity in Syria and Persia through the Semitic dialect known as Aramaic, by which Greek and Persian culture had been transmitted to the Arabs before the rise of Islam. In this case, as in many others, the history of language runs on parallel lines with the history of civilisation. The necessities of increasing civilisation had introduced many Aramaic words to the Arabic vocabulary before Muhammed's day: these importations increased considerably when the Arabs entered a wider and more complex civilisation and were especially considerable where intellectual culture was concerned. Even Greek terms made their way into Arabic through Aramaic. This natural dependency of Arabic upon Aramaic, which in turn was connected with Greek as the rival Christian vernacular in these regions, is alone sufficient evidence that Christianity exerted a direct influence upon Muhammedanism. Moreover, as we have seen, the Qoran itself regarded Christians as being in possession of divine wisdom, and some reference both to Christianity and to Judaism was necessary to explain the many unintelligible passages of the Qoran. Allusions were made to texts and statements in the Thora and the Gospels, and God was represented as constantly appealing to earlier revelations of Himself. Thus it was only natural that interpreters should study these scriptures and ask counsel of their possessors. Of primary importance was the fact that both Christians and Jews, and the former in particular, accepted Muhammedanism by thousands, and formed a new intellectual class of ability infinitely superior to that of the original Muslims and able to attract the best elements of the Arab nationality to their teaching. It was as impossible for these apostate Christians to abandon their old habits of thought as it was hopeless to expect any sudden change in the economic conditions under which they lived. Christian theories of God and the world naturally assumed a Muhammedan colouring and thus the great process of accommodating Christianity to Muhammedanism was achieved. The Christian contribution to this end was made partly directly and partly by teaching, and in the intellectual as well as in the economic sphere the ultimate ideal was inevitably dictated by the superior culture of Christianity. The Muhammedans were thus obliged to accept Christian hypotheses on theological points and the fundaments of Christian and Muhammedan culture thus become identical. I use the term hypotheses, for the reason that the final determination of the points at issue was by no means identical, wherever the Qoran definitely contradicted Christian views of morality or social laws. But in these cases also, Christian ideas were able to impose themselves upon tradition and to issue in practice, even when opposed by the actual text of the Qoran. They did not always pass unquestioned and even on trivial points were obliged to encounter some resistance. The theory of the Sunday was accepted, but that day was not chosen and Friday was preferred: meetings for worship were held in imitation of Christian practice, but attempts to sanctify the day and to proclaim it a day of rest were forbidden: except for the performance of divine service, Friday was an ordinary week-day. When, however, the Qoran was in any sort of harmony with Christianity, the Christian ideas of the age were textually accepted in any further development of the question. The fact is obvious, not only as regards details, but also in the general theory of man's position upon earth.

* * * * *

Muhammed, the preacher of repentance, had become a temporal prince in Medina; his civil and political administration was ecclesiastical in character, an inevitable result of his position as the apostle of God, whose congregation was at the same time a state. This theory of the state led later theorists unconsciously to follow the lead of Christianity, which regarded the church as supreme in every department of life, and so induced Muhammedanism to adopt views of life and social order which are now styled mediaeval. The theological development of this system is to be attributed chiefly to groups of pious thinkers in Medina: they were excluded from political life when the capital was transferred from Medina to Damascus and were left in peace to elaborate their theory of the Muhammedan divine polity. The influence of these groups was paramount: but of almost equal importance was the influence of the proselytes in the conquered lands who were Christians for the most part and for that reason far above their Arab contemporaries in respect of intellectual training and culture. We find that the details of jurisprudence, dogma, and mysticism can only be explained by reference to Christian stimulus, nor is it any exaggeration to ascribe the further development of Muhammed's views to the influence of thinkers who regarded the religious polity of Islam as the realisation of an ideal which

Christianity had hitherto vainly striven to attain. This ideal was the supremacy of religion over life and all its activities, over the state and the individual alike. But it was a religion primarily concerned with the next world, where alone real worth was to be found. Earthly life was a pilgrimage to be performed and earthly intentions had no place with heavenly. The joy of life which the ancient world had known, art, music and culture, all were rejected or valued only as aids to religion. Human action was judged with reference only to its appraisement in the life to come. That ascetic spirit was paramount, which had enchained the Christian world, that renunciation of secular affairs which explains the peculiar methods by which mediaeval views of life found expression. Asceticism did not disturb the course of life as a whole. It might condemn but it could not suppress the natural impulse of man to propagate his race: it might hamper economic forces, but it could not destroy them. It eventually led to a compromise in every department of life, but for centuries it retained its domination over men's minds and to some material extent over their actions.

Such was the environment in which Islam was planted: its deepest roots had been fertilised with Christian theory, and in spite of Muhammed's call to repentance, its most characteristic manifestations were somewhat worldly and non-ascetic. "Islam knows not monasticism" says the tradition which this tendency produced. The most important compromise of all, that with life, which Christianity only secured by gradual steps, had been already attained for Islam by Muhammed himself and was included in the course of his development. As Islam

now entered the Christian world, it was forced to
pass through this process of development once
more. At the outset it was permeated with the idea
of Christian asceticism, to which an inevitable
opposition arose, and found expression in such
statements as that already quoted. But Muhammed's
preaching had obviously striven to honour the
future life by painting the actual world in the
gloomiest colours, and the material optimism of the
secular-minded was unable to check the advance of
Christian asceticism among the classes which felt a
real interest in religion. Hence that surprising
similarity of views upon the problem of existence,
which we have now to outline. In details of outward
form great divergency is apparent. Christianity
possessed a clergy while Islam did not: yet the force
of Christian influence produced a priestly class in
Islam. It was a class acting not as mediator between
God and man through sacraments and mysteries, but
as moral leaders and legal experts; as such it was no
less important than the scribes under Judaism.
Unanimity among these scholars could produce
decisions no less binding than those of the Christian
clergy assembled in church councils. They are
representatives of the congregation which "has no
unanimity, for such would be an error." Islam
naturally preferred to adopt unanimous conclusions
in silence rather than to vote in assemblies. As a
matter of fact a body of orthodox opinion was
developed by this means with no less success than
in Christendom. Any agreement which the quiet
work of the scholars had secured upon any question
was ratified by God and was thus irrevocably and
eternally binding. For instance, the proclamation to
the faithful of new ideas upon the exposition of the

Qoran or of tradition was absolutely forbidden; the scholars, in other words the clergy, had convinced themselves, by the fact of their unanimity upon the point, that the customary and traditional mode of exposition was the one pleasing to God. Ideas of this kind naturally remind us of Roman Catholic practice. The influence of Eastern Christianity upon Islam is undoubtedly visible here. This influence could not in the face of Muhammedan tradition and custom, create an organised clergy, but it produced a clerical class to guard religious thought, and as religion spread, to supervise thought of every kind. Christianity again condemned marriage, though it eventually agreed to a compromise sanctifying this tie; Islam, on the contrary, found in the Qoran the text "Ye that are unmarried shall marry" (24, 32). In the face of so clear a statement, the condemnation of marriage, which in any case was contrary to the whole spirit of the Qoran, could not be maintained. Thus the Muhammedan tradition contains numerous sayings in support of marriage. "A childless house contains no blessing": "the breath of a son is as the breath of Paradise"; "when a man looks upon his wife (in love) and she upon him, God looks down in mercy upon them both." "Two prayers of a married man are more precious in the sight of God than seventy of a bachelor." With many similar variations upon the theme, Muhammed is said to have urged marriage upon his followers. On the other hand an almost equally numerous body of warnings against marriage exists, also issued by Muhammed. I know no instance of direct prohibition, but serious admonitions are found which usually take the form of denunciation of the female sex and were early interpreted as warnings

by tradition. "Fear the world and women": "thy
worst enemies are the wife at thy side and thy
concubine": "the least in Paradise are the women":
"women are the faggots of hell"; "pious women are
rare as ravens with white or red legs and white
beaks"; "but for women men might enter Paradise."
Here we come upon a strain of thought especially
Christian. Muhammed regarded the satisfaction of
the sexual instincts as natural and right and made no
attempt to put restraint upon it: Christian asceticism
regarded this impulse as the greatest danger which
could threaten the spiritual life of its adherents, and
the sentences above quoted may be regarded as the
expression of this view. Naturally the social
position of the woman suffered in consequence and
is so much worse in the traditional
Muhammedanism as compared with the Qoran that
the change can only be ascribed to the influence of
the civilisation which the Muhammedans
encountered. The idea of woman as a creature of no
account is certainly rooted in the ancient East, but it
reached Islam in Christian dress and with the
authority of Christian hostility to marriage.
With this hostility to marriage are probably
connected the regulations concerning the covering
of the body: in the ancient church only the face, the
hands and the feet were to be exposed to view, the
object being to prevent the suggestion of sinful
thoughts: it is also likely that objections to the
ancient habit of leaving the body uncovered found
expression in this ordinance. Similar objections may
be found in Muhammedan tradition; we may regard
these as further developments of commands given
in the Qoran, but it is also likely that Muhammed's
apocryphal statements upon the point were dictated

by Christian religious theory. They often appear in connection with warnings against frequenting the public baths, which fact is strong evidence of their Christian origin. "A bad house is the bath: much turmoil is therein and men show their nakedness." "Fear that house that is called the bathhouse and if any enter therein, let him veil himself." "He who believes in God and the last Judgment, let him enter the bath only in bathing dress." "Nakedness is forbidden to us." There is a story of the prophet, to the effect that he was at work unclothed when a voice from heaven ordered him to cover his nakedness!

* * * * *

We thus see, that an astonishing similarity is apparent in the treatment even of questions where divergency is fundamental. Divergency, it is true, existed, but pales before the general affinity of the two theories of life. Our judgment upon Christian medievalism in this respect can be applied directly and literally to Muhammedanism. Either religion regards man as no more than a sojourner in this world. It is not worth while to arrange for a permanent habitation, and luxurious living is but pride. Hence the simplicity of private dwellings in mediaeval times both in the East and West. Architectural expense is confined to churches and mosques, which were intended for the service of God. These Christian ideas are reflected in the inexhaustible storehouse of Muhammedan theory, the great collections of tradition, as follows. "The worst use which a believer can make of his money is to build." "Every building, except a mosque, will stand to the discredit of its architect on the day of resurrection." These polemics which Islam inherited

from Christianity are directed not only against
building in general, but also against the erection and
decoration of lofty edifices: "Should a man build a
house nine ells high, a voice will call to him from
heaven, Whither wilt thou rise, most profane of the
profane?" "No prophet enters a house adorned with
fair decoration." With these prohibitions should be
connected the somewhat unintelligible fact that the
most pious Caliphs sat upon thrones (*mimbar*,
"president's chair") of clay. The simplest and most
transitory material thus serves to form the symbol of
temporal power. A house is adorned not by outward
show, but by the fact that prayer is offered and the
Qoran recited within its walls. These theories were
out of harmony with the worldly tendencies of the
conquerors, who built themselves castles, such as
Qusair Amra: they belong to the spirit of
Christianity rather than to Islam.

Upon similar principles we may explain the demand
for the utmost simplicity and reserve in regard to
the other enjoyments of life. To eat whenever one
may wish is excess and two meals a day are more
than enough. The portion set apart for one may also
suffice for two. Ideas of this kind are of constant
recurrence in the Muhammedan traditions:
indispensable needs alone are to be satisfied, as
indeed Thomas Aquinas teaches. Similar
observations apply to dress: "he who walks in costly
garments to be seen of men is not seen of the Lord."
Gold and silver ornaments, and garments of purple
and silk are forbidden by both religions. Princes
live as simply as beggars and possess only one
garment, so that they are unable to appear in public
when it is being washed: they live upon a handful of
dates and are careful to save paper and artificial

light. Such incidents are common in the oldest records of the first Caliphs. These princes did not, of course, live in such beggary, and the fact is correspondingly important that after the lapse of one or two generations the Muhammedan historians should describe their heroes as possessing only the typical garment of the Christian saint. This one fact speaks volumes.

Every action was performed in God or with reference to God--an oft-repeated idea in either religion. There is a continual hatred of the world and a continual fear that it may imperil a man's soul. Hence the sense of vast responsibility felt by the officials, a sense which finds expression even in the ordinary official correspondence of the authorities which papyri have preserved for us. The phraseology is often stereotyped, but as such, expresses a special theory of life. This responsibility is represented as weighing with especial severity upon a pious Caliph. Upon election to the throne he accepts office with great reluctance protesting his unworthiness with tears. The West can relate similar stories of Gregory the Great and of Justinian.

Exhortations are frequent ever to remember the fact of death and to repent and bewail past sins. When a mention of the last Judgment occurs in the reading of passages from the Bible or Qoran, the auditors burst into tears. Upon one occasion a man was praying upon the roof of his house and wept so bitterly over his sins, that the tears ran down the waterspout and flooded the rooms below. This hyperbolical statement in a typical life of a saint shows the high value attributed to tears in the East. It is, however, equally a Christian characteristic.

The gracious gift of tears was regarded by mediaeval Christianity as the sign of a deeply religious nature. Gregory VII is said to have wept daily at the sacrifice of the Mass and similar accounts are given to the credit of other famous Christians.

While a man should weep for his own sins, he is not to bewail any misfortune or misery which may befall him. In the latter case it is his duty to collect his strength, to resign himself and to praise God even amid his sufferings. Should he lose a dear relative by death, he is not to break out with cries and lamentations like the heathen. Lamentation for the dead is most strictly forbidden in Islam. "We are God's people and to God we return" says the pious Muslim on receiving the unexpected news of a death. Resignation and patience in these matters is certainly made the subject of eloquent exhortation in the Qoran, but the special developments of tradition betray Christian influence.

Generally speaking, the whole ethical system of the two religions is based upon the contrast between God and the world, though Muhammedan philosophy will recognize no principle beside that of God. As a typical example we may take a sentence from the Spanish bishop Isidor who died in 636: "Good are the intentions directed towards God and bad are those directed to earthly gain or transitory fame." Any Muhammedan theologian would have subscribed to this statement. On the one hand stress is laid upon motive as giving its value to action. The first sentence in the most famous collection of traditions runs, "Deeds shall be judged by their intentions." On the other hand is the contrast between God and the world, or as Islam puts it, between the present and the future life. The Christian gains eternal life by following Christ. Imitation of the Master in all things even to the stigmata, is the characteristic feature of mediaeval Christianity. Nor is the whole of the so-called Sunna obedience anything more than the imitation of Muhammed which seeks to repeat the smallest details of his life. The infinite importance attached by Islam to the Sunna seems to me to have originated in Christian influence. The development of it betrays original features, but the fundamental principle is Christian, as all the leading ideas of Islam are Christian, in the sense of the term as paraphrased above. Imitation of Christ in the first instance, attempts to repeat his poverty and renunciation of personal property: this is the great Christian ideal. Muhammed was neither poor nor without possessions: at the end of his life he had become a prince and had directly stated that property was a gift from God. In spite of that his successors praise poverty and their praises were the best of evidence that they were influenced not by the prophet himself but by Christianity. While the traditions are full of the praises of poverty and the dangers of wealth, assertions in praise of wealth also occur, for the reason that the pure Muhammedan ideas opposed to Christianity retained a certain influence. J. Goldziher has published an interesting study showing how many words borrowed from this source occur in the written Muhammedan traditions: an almost complete version of the Lord's Prayer is quoted. Even the idea of love towards enemies, which would have been unintelligible to Muhammed, made its way into the traditions: "the most virtuous of acts is to seek out him who rejects thee, to give to him that despises thee and to pardon him that oppresses thee." The Gospel precept to do unto others as we would they should do unto us (Matt. vii. 12, Luke vi. 31) is to be found in the Arab traditions, and many similar points of contact may be noticed. A man's "neighbour" has ever been, despite the teaching of Jesus, to the Christian and to the Muhammedan, his co-religionist. The whole department of Muhammedan ethics has thus been subjected to strong Christian influence.

Naturally this ecclesiasticism which dominated the whole of life, was bound to assert itself in state organisation. An abhorrence of the state, so far as it was independent of religion, a feeling unknown in the ancient world, pervades both Christianity and Muhammedanism, Christianity first struggled to secure recognition in the state and afterwards fought with the state for predominance. Islam and the state were at first identical: in its spiritual leaders it was soon separated from the state. Its idea of a divine polity was elaborated to the smallest details, but remained a theory which never became practice. Yet this ideal retained such strength that every Muhammedan usurper was careful to secure his investiture by the Caliph, the nominal leader of this ecclesiastical state, even if force were necessary to attain his object. For instance, Saladin was absolutely independent of the nominal Caliph in Bagdad, but could not feel that his position was secure until he had obtained his sultan's patent from the Caliph. Only then did his supremacy rest upon a religious basis and he was not regarded by popular opinion as a legitimate monarch until this ceremony had been performed. This theory corresponds with constitutional ideals essentially Christian. "The tyranny," wrote Innocent IV to the Emperor Frederick II, "which was once generally exercised throughout the world, was resigned into the hands of the Church by Constantine, who then received as an honourable gift from the proper source that which he had formerly held and exercised unrighteously." The long struggle between Church and State in this matter is well known. In this struggle the rising power of Islam had adopted a similar attitude. The great abhorrence of a secular "monarchy" in opposition to a religious caliphate, as expressed both by the dicta of tradition and by the Abbassid historians, was inspired, in my opinion, by Christian dislike of a divorce between Church and State. The phenomenon might be explained without reference to external influence, but if the whole process be considered in connection, Christian influence seems more than probable.

A similar attitude was also assumed by either religion towards the facts of economic life. In either case the religious point of view is characteristic. The reaction against the tendency to condemn secular life is certainly stronger in Islam, but is also apparent in Christianity. Thomas Aquinas directly stigmatises trade as a disgraceful means of gain, because the exchange of wares does not necessitate labour or the satisfaction of necessary wants: Muhammedan tradition says, "The pious merchant is a pioneer on the road of God." "The first to enter Paradise is the honourable merchant." Here the solution given to the problem differs in either case, but in Christian practice, opposition was also obvious. Common to both religions is the condemnation of the exaction of interest and monetary speculation, which the middle ages regarded as usury. Islam, as usual, gives this Christian idea the form of a saying enounced by Muhammed: "He who speculates in grain for forty days, grinds and bakes it and gives it to the poor, makes an offering unacceptable to God." "He who raises prices to Muslims (by speculation) will be cast head downwards by God into the hottest fire of hell." Many similar traditions fulminate against usury in the widest sense of the word. These prohibitions were circumvented in practice by deed of gift and exchange, but none the less the free development of commercial enterprise was hampered by these fetters which modern civilisation first broke. Enterprise was thus confined to agriculture under these circumstances both for Christianity and Islam, and economic life in either case became "mediaeval" in outward appearance. Methods of making profit without a proportional expenditure of labour were the particular objects of this aversion. Manual labour was highly esteemed both in the East and West. A man's first duty was to support himself by the work of his own hands, a duty proclaimed, as we know, from the apostolic age onwards. So far as Islam is concerned, this view may be illustrated by the following utterances: "The best of deeds is the gain of that which is lawful": "the best gain is made by sale within lawful limits and by manual labour." "The most precious gain is that made by manual labour; that which a man thus earns and gives to himself, his people, his sons and his servants, is as meritorious as alms." Thus practical work is made incumbent upon the believer, and the extent to which manufacture flourished in East and West during the middle ages is well known.

A similar affinity is apparent as regards ideas upon social position and occupation. Before God man is but a slave: even the mighty Caliphs themselves, even those who were stigmatised by posterity as secular monarchs, included in their official titles the designation, "slave of God." This theory was carried out into the smallest details of life, even into those which modern observers would consider as unconcerned with religion. Thus at meals the Muslim was not allowed to recline at table, an ancient custom which the upper classes had followed for centuries: he must sit, "as a slave," according to the letter of the law. All are alike slaves, for the reason that they are believers: hence the humiliation of those whom chance has exalted is thought desirable. This idealism is undoubtedly more deeply rooted in the popular consciousness of the East than of the West. In the East great social distinctions occur; but while religion recognises them, it forbids insistence upon them.

As especially distinctive of social work in either religion we might be inclined to regard the unparalleled extent of organizations for the care of the poor, for widows and orphans, for the old, infirm and sick, the public hospitals and almshouses and religious foundations in the widest sense of the term; but the object of these activities was not primarily social nor were they undertaken to make life easier for the poor: religious selfishness was the leading motive, the desire to purify self by good works and to secure the right to pre-eminence in heaven. "For the salvation of my soul and for everlasting reward" is the formula of many a

Christian foundation deed. Very similar expressions of hope for eternal reward occur in Muhammedan deeds of gift. A foundation inscription on a mosque, published by E. Littmann, is stated in terms the purport of which is unmistakable. "This has been built by N or M: may a house be built for him in Paradise (in return)." Here again, the idea of the house in Paradise is borrowed from Christian ideas. We have already observed that in Islam the smallest trivialities of daily life become matters of religious import. The fact is especially apparent in a wide department of personal conduct. Islam certainly went to further extremes than Christianity in this matter, but these customs are clearly only further developments of Christian regulations. The call to simplicity of food and dress has already been mentioned. But even the simplest food was never to be taken before thanks had been given to God: grace was never to be omitted either before or after meals. Divine ordinances also regulated the manner of eating. The prophet said, "With one finger the devils eat, with two the Titans of antiquity and with three fingers the prophets." The application of the saying is obvious. Similar sayings prescribe the mode of handling dishes and behaviour at a common meal, if the blessing of God is to be secured. There seems to be a Christian touch in one of these rules which runs, in the words of the prophet: "He who picks up the crumbs fallen from the table and eats them, will be forgiven by God." "He who licks the empty dishes and his fingers will be filled by God here and in the world to come." "When a man licks the dish from which he has eaten, the dish will plead for him before God." I regard these words as practical applications of the

text, "Gather up the pieces that remain, that nothing
be lost" (Matt. xiv. 10: John vi. 12). Even to-day
South Italians kiss bread that has fallen to the
ground, in order to make apology to the gift of God.
Volumes might be filled with rules of polite
manners in this style: hardly any detail is to be
found in the whole business of daily life, even
including occupations regarded as unclean, which
was not invested with some religious significance.
These rules are almost entirely dictated by the spirit
of early Christianity and it is possible to reconstruct
the details of life in those dark ages from these
literary records which are now the only source of
evidence upon such points. However, we must here
content ourselves with establishing the fact that
Islam adopted Christian practice in this as in other
departments of life.

The state, society, the individual, economics and
morality were thus collectively under Christian
influence during the early period of
Muhammedanism. Conditions very similar in
general, affected those conceptions which we
explain upon scientific grounds but which were
invariably regarded by ancient and mediaeval
thought as supernatural, conceptions deduced from
the phenomena of illness and dreams. Islam was no
less opposed than Christianity to the practice of
magic in any form, but only so far as these practices
seemed to preserve remnants of heathen beliefs.
Such beliefs were, however, continued in both
religions in modified form. There is no doubt that
ideas of high antiquity, doubtless of Babylonian
origin, can be traced as contributing to the
formation of these beliefs, while scientific medicine
is connected with the earlier discoveries of Greece.

Common to both religions was the belief in the reality of dreams, especially when these seemed to harmonise with religious ideas: dreams were regarded as revelations from God or from his apostles or from the pious dead. The fact that man could dream and that he could appear to other men in dreams after his death was regarded as a sign of divine favour and the biographies of the saints often contain chapters devoted to this faculty. These are natural ideas which lie in the national consciousness of any people, but owe their development in the case of Islam to Christian influence. The same may be said of the belief that the prayers of particular saints were of special efficacy, and of attempts by prayer, forms of worship and the like to procure rain, avert plague and so forth: such ideas are common throughout the middle ages. Thus in every department we meet with that particular type of Christian theory which existed in the East during the seventh and eighth centuries.

This mediaeval theory of life was subjected, as is well known, to many compromises in the West, and was materially modified by Teutonic influence and the revival of classicism. It might therefore be supposed that in Islam Christian theory underwent similar modification or disappeared entirely. But the fact is not so. At the outset, we stated, as will be remembered, that Muhammedan scholars were accustomed to propound their dicta as utterances given by Muhammed himself, and in this form Christian ideas also came into circulation among Muhammedans. When attempts were made to systematise these sayings, all were treated as alike authentic, and, as traditional, exerted their share of influence upon the formation of canon law. Thus questions of temporary importance to mediaeval Christianity became permanent elements in Muhammedan theology.

One highly instructive instance may be given. During the century which preceded the Byzantine iconoclastic controversy, the whole of nearer Asia was disturbed by the question whether the erection and veneration of images was permissible. That Constantinople attempted to prohibit such veneration is well known: but after a long struggle the church gained its wishes. Islam was confronted with the problem and decided for prohibition, doubtless under Jewish influence. Sayings of Muhammed forbid the erection of images. This prohibition became part of canon law and therefore binding for all time: it remains obligatory at the present day, though in practice it is often transgressed. Thus the process of development which was continued in Christendom, came to a standstill in Islam, and many similar cases might be quoted.

Here begins the development of Muhammedan jurisprudence or, more exactly, of the doctrine of duty, which includes every kind of human activity, duties to God and man, religion, civil law, the penal code, social morality and economics. This extraordinary system of moral obligations, as developed in Islam, though its origin is obscure, is doubtless rooted in the ecclesiastical law of Christendom which was then first evolved. I have no doubt that the development of Muhammedan tradition, which precedes the code proper, was dependent upon the growth of canon law in the old Church, and that this again, or at least the purely legal part of it, is closely connected with the pre-

Justinian legislation. Roman law does not seem to me to have influenced Islam immediately in the form of Justinian's *Corpus Juris*, but indirectly from such ecclesiastical sources as the Romano-Syrian code. This view, however, I would distinctly state, is merely my conjecture. For our present purpose it is more important to establish the fact that the doctrine of duty canonised the manifold expressions of the theory that life is a religion, with which we have met throughout the traditional literature: all human acts are thus legally considered as obligatory or forbidden when corresponding with religious commands or prohibitions, as congenial or obnoxious to the law or as matters legally indifferent and therefore permissible. The arrangement of the work of daily life in correspondence with these religious points of view is the most important outcome of the Muhammedan doctrine of duties. The religious utterances which also cover the whole business of life were first made duties by this doctrine: in practice their fulfilment is impossible, but the theory of their obligatory nature is a fundamental element in Muhammedanism.

Where the doctrine of duties deals with legal rights, its application was in practice confined to marriage and the affairs of family life: the theoretical demands of its penal clauses, for instance, raise impossible difficulties. At the same time, it has been of great importance to the whole spiritual life of Islam down to the present day, because it reflects Muhammedan ideals of life and of man's place in the world. Even to-day it remains the daily bread of the soul that desires instruction, to quote the words of the greatest father of the Muhammedan church. It

will thus be immediately obvious to what a vast
extent Christian theory of the seventh and eighth
centuries still remains operative upon
Muhammedan thought throughout the world.
Considerable parts of the doctrine of duties are
concerned with the forms of Muhammedan
worship. It is becoming ever clearer that only slight
tendencies to a form of worship were apparent
under Muhammed. The mosque, the building
erected for the special purpose of divine service,
was unknown during the prophet's lifetime; nor was
there any definite church organisation, of which the
most important parts are the common ritual and the
preaching. Tendencies existed but no system, was to
be found: there was no clerical class to take an
interest in the development of an order of divine
service. The Caliphs prayed before the faithful in
the capital, as did the governors in the provinces.
The military commanders also led a simple service
in their own stations.

It was contact with foreign influence which first
provided the impulse to a systematic form of
worship. Both Christians and Jews possessed such
forms. Their example was followed and a ritual was
evolved, at first of the very simplest kind. No
detailed organisation, however, was attempted, until
Christian influence led to the formation of the class
which naturally took an interest in the matter, the
professional theologians. These soon replaced the
military service leaders. This change denoted the
final stage in the development of ritual. The object
of the theologians was to subject the various
occupations of life to ritual as well as to religion.
The mediatorial or sacramental theories of the
priestly office were unknown to Islam, but ritual

customs of similar character were gradually evolved, and are especially pronounced in the ceremonies of marriage and burial.

More important, however, was the development of the official service, the arrangement of the day and the hour of obligatory attendance and the introduction of preaching: under Muhammed and his early followers, and until late in the Omajjad period, preaching was confined to addresses, given as occasion demanded, but by degrees it became part of the regular ritual. With it was afterwards connected the intercession for the Caliphs, which became a highly significant part of the service, as symbolising their sovereignty. It seems to me very probable that this practice was an adoption, at any rate in theory, of the Christian custom of praying for the emperor. The pulpit was then introduced under Christian influence, which thus completely transformed the chair (_mimbar_) of the ancient Arab judges and rulers and made it a piece of church furniture; the Christian *cancelli* or choir screens were adopted and the mosque was thus developed. Before the age of mosques, a lance had been planted in the ground and prayer offered behind it: so in the mosque a prayer niche was made, a survival of the pre-existing custom. There are many obscure points in the development of the worship, but one fact may be asserted with confidence: the developments of ritual were derived from pre-existing practices, which were for the most part Christian.

But the religious energy of Islam was not exclusively devoted to the development and practice of the doctrine of duties; at the same time this ethical department, in spite of its dependency upon Christian and Jewish ideas, remains its most original achievement: we have pursued the subject at some length, because its importance is often overlooked in the course of attempts to estimate the connection between Christianity and Islam. On the other hand, affinities in the regions of mysticism and dogma have long been matter of common knowledge and a brief sketch of them will therefore suffice. If not essential to our purpose within the limits of this book, they are none the less necessary to complete our treatment of the subject.

By mysticism we understand the expression of religious emotion, as contrasted with efforts to attain righteousness by full obedience to the ethical doctrine of duties, and also in contrast to the hair-splitting of dogmatic speculation: mysticism strove to reach immediate emotional unity with the Godhead. No trace of any such tendency was to be found in the Qoran: it entered Islam as a complete novelty, and the affinities which enabled it to gain a footing have been difficult to trace.

Muhammedan mysticism is certainly not exclusively Christian: its origins, like those of Christian mysticism, are to be found in the pantheistic writings of the Neoplatonist school of Dionysius the Areopagite: but Islam apparently derived its mysticism from Christian sources. In it originated the idea, with all its capacity for development, of the mystical love of God: to this was added the theory and practice of asceticism which was especially developed by Christianity, and, in later times, the influence of Indian philosophy, which is unmistakable. Such are the fundamental elements of this tendency. When the idea of the Nirwana, the Arab _fan[=a]_, is attained,

Muhammedanism proper comes to an end. But orthodoxy controls the divergent elements: it opposes any open avowal of the logical conclusion, which would identify "God" and the "ego," but in practice this group of ideas, pantheistic in all but name, has been received and given a place side by side with the strict monotheism of the Qoran and with the dogmatic theology. Any form of mysticism which is pushed to its logical consequences must overthrow positive religion. By incorporating this dangerous tendency within itself, Islam has averted the peril which it threatens. Creed is no longer endangered, and this purpose being secured, thought is free.

Union with God is gained by ecstasy and leads to enthusiasm. These terms will therefore show us in what quarter we must seek the strongest impulses to mysticism. The concepts, if not the actual terms, are to be found in Islam: they were undoubtedly transmitted by Christianity and undergo the wide extension which results in the dervish and fakir developments. *Dervish* and *fakir* are the Persian and Arabic words for "beggar": the word *sufi*, a man in a woollen shirt, is also used in the same sense. The terms show that asceticism is a fundamental element in mysticism; asceticism was itself an importation to Islam. Dervishes are divided into different classes or orders, according to the methods by which they severally prefer to attain ecstasy: dancing and recitation are practised by the dancing and howling dervishes and other methods are in vogue. It is an institution very different from monasticism but the result of a course of development undoubtedly similar to that which produced the monk: dervishism and monasticism are independent developments of the same original idea.

Among these Muhammedan companies attempts to reach the point of ecstasy have developed to a rigid discipline of the soul; the believer must subject himself to his master, resigning all power of will, and so gradually reaches higher stages of knowledge until he is eventually led to the consciousness of his absolute identity with God. It seems to me beyond question that this method is reflected in the *exercitiis spiritualibus* of Ignatius Loyola, the chief instrument by which the Jesuits secured dominion over souls. Any one who has realised the enormous influence which Arab thought exerted upon Spanish Christianity so late as the fourteenth and fifteenth centuries, will not regard the conjecture as unfounded.

When a man's profession or position prevented him from practising these mystical exercises, he satisfied his religious needs by venerating persons who were nearer to the deity and whose intercession was effectual even after their death and sometimes not until they were dead: hence arose the veneration of saints, a practice as alien as pantheistic dogma to primitive Islam. The adoption of Christian saint worship was not possible until the person of Muhammed himself had been exalted above the ordinary level of humanity. Early Muhammedans observed that the founder of Christianity was regarded by popular opinion as a miracle worker of unrivalled power: it was impossible for the founder of Islam to remain inferior in this respect. Thus the early biographies of the prophet, which appeared in the first century of Muhammedanism, recount the typical miracles of the Gospels, the feeding of multitudes, healing the sick, raising the dead and so forth. Two methods of adoption may be distinguished. Special features are directly borrowed, or the line of advance is followed which had introduced the worship of saints and relics to Christianity a short time before. The religious emotions natural to any people produced a series of ideas which pass from one religion to another. Outward form and purport may be changed, but the essential points remain unaltered and are the living expression of that relation to God in which a people conceives itself to stand. Higher forms of religion-- a fact as sad as it is true--require a certain degree not only of moral but of intellectual capacity.

Thus we have traversed practically the whole circle of religious life and have everywhere found Islam following in the path of Christian thought. One department remains to be examined, which might be expected to offer but scanty opportunity for borrowings of this kind; this is dogma. Here, if anywhere, the contrast between the two religions should be obvious. The initial divergencies were so pronounced, that any adoption of Christian ideas would seem impossible. Yet in those centuries, Christianity was chiefly agitated by dogmatic questions, which occupied men's minds as greatly as social problems at the present day. Here we can observe most distinctly, how the problems at least were taken over by Islam.

Muhammedan dogmatic theology is concerned only with three main questions, the problem of free-will, the being and attributes of God, and the eternal uncreated nature of God's word. The mere mention of these problems will recall the great dogmatic struggles of early Christianity. At no time have the problems of free-will and the nature of God, been subjects of fiercer dispute than during the Christological and subsequent discussions. Upholders of freedom or of determinism could alike find much to support their theories in the Qoran: Muhammed was no dogmatist and for him the ideas of man's responsibility and of God's almighty and universal power were not mutually exclusive. The statement of the problem was adopted from Christianity as also was the dialectical subtlety by which a solution was reached, and which, while admitting the almighty power of God, left man responsible for his deeds by regarding him as free to accept or refuse the admonitions of God. Thus the thinkers and their demands for justice and righteous dealing were reconciled to the blind fatalism of the masses, which again was not a native Muhammedan product, but is the outcome of the religious spirit of the East.

The problem of reconciling the attributes of God with the dogma of His unity was solved with no less subtlety. The mere idea that a multiplicity of attributes was incompatible with absolute unity was only possible in a school which had spent centuries in the desperate attempt to reconcile the inference of a divine Trinity with the conception of absolute divine unity.

Finally, the third question, "Was the Qoran, the word of God, created or not?" is an obvious counterpart of the Logos problem, of the struggle to secure recognition of the Logos as eternal and uncreated together with God. Islam solved the question by distinguishing the eternal and uncreated Qoran from the revealed and created. The eternal nature of the Qoran was a dogma entirely alien to

the strict monotheism of Islam: but this fact was
never realised, any more than the fact that the
acceptance of the dogma was a triumph for Graeco-
Christian dialectic. There can be no more striking
proof of the strength of Christian influence: it was
able to undermine the fundamental dogma of Islam,
and the Muhammedans never realised the fact.

In our review of these dogmatic questions, we have
met with a novel tendency, that to metaphysical
speculation and dialectic. It was from Christendom,
not directly from the Greek world, that this spirit
reached Islam: the first attitude of Muhammedanism
towards it was that which Christianity adopted
towards all non-religious systems of thought. Islam
took it up as a useful weapon for the struggle
against heresy. But it soon became a favourite and
trusted implement and eventually its influence upon
Muhammedan philosophy became paramount. Here
we meet with a further Christian influence, which,
when once accepted, very largely contributed to
secure a similar development of mediaeval
Christian and Muhammedan thought. This was
Scholasticism, which was the natural and inevitable
consequence of the study of Greek dialectic and
philosophy. It is not necessary to sketch the growth
of scholasticism, with its barrenness of results in
spite of its keen intellectual power, upon ground
already fertilised by ecclesiastical pioneers. It will
suffice to state the fact that these developments of
the Greek spirit were predominant here as in the
West: in either case important philosophies rise
upon this basis, for the most part professedly
ecclesiastical, even when they occasionally struck at
the roots of the religious system to which they
belonged. In this department, Islam repaid part of

its debt to Christianity, for the Arabs became the intellectual leaders of the middle ages.

Thus we come to the concluding section of this treatise; before we enter upon it, two preliminary questions remain for consideration. If Islam was ready to learn from Christianity in every department of religious life, what was the cause of the sudden superiority of Muhammedanism to the rising force of Christianity a few centuries later? And secondly, in view of the traditional antagonism between the Christian and Muhammedan worlds, how was Christianity able to adopt so large and essential a portion of Muhammedan thought?

The answer in the second case will be clear to any one who has followed our argument with attention. The intellectual and religious outlook was so similar in both religions and the problem requiring solution so far identical that nothing existed to impede the adoption of ideas originally Christian which had been developed in the East. The fact that the West could accept philosophical and theological ideas from Islam and that an actual interchange of thought could proceed in this direction, is the best of proofs for the soundness of our argument that the roots of Muhammedanism are to be sought in Christianity. Islam was able to borrow from Christianity for the reason that Muhammed's ideas were derived from that source: similarly Christianity was able to turn Arab thought to its own purposes because that thought was founded upon Christian principles. The sources of both religions lie in the East and in Oriental thought. No less is true of Judaism, a scholastic system which was excellently adapted by its international character, to become a medium of communication between Christianity and Muhammedanism during those centuries. In this connection special mention must be made of the Spanish Jews; to their work, not only as transmitting but also as originating ideas a bare reference must here suffice. But of greater importance was the direct exchange of thought, which proceeded through literary channels, by means of translations, especially by word of mouth among the Christians and Muhammedans who were living together in Southern Italy, Sicily, and Spain, and by commercial intercourse.

The other question concerns the fundamental problem of European medievalism. We see that the problems with which the middle ages in Europe were confronted and also that European ethics and metaphysics were identical with the Muhammedan system: we are moreover assured that the acceptance of Christian ideas by Islam can only have taken place in the East: and the conclusion is obvious that mediaeval Christianity was also primarily rooted in the East. The transmission of this religious philosophy to the non-Oriental peoples of the West at first produced a cessation of progress but opened a new intellectual world when these peoples awoke to life in the thirteenth and fourteenth centuries. But throughout the intermediate period between the seventh and thirteenth centuries the East was gaining political strength and was naturally superior to the West where political organisation and culture had been shattered by the Germanic invasions; in the East again there was an organic unity of national strength and intellectual ideals, as the course of development had not been interrupted. Though special dogmatic points had been changed, the general religious theory remained unaltered throughout the nearer East. Thus the rising power of Islam, which had high faculties of self-accommodation to environment, was able to enter upon the heritage of the mixed Graeco-Oriental civilisation existing in the East; in consequence it gained an immediate advantage over the West, where Eastern ideas were acclimatised with difficulty.

The preponderance of Muhammedan influence was increased by the fact that Islam became the point of amalgamation for ancient Eastern cultures, in particular for those of Greece and Persia: in previous centuries preparation had been made for this process by the steady transformation of Hellenism to Orientalism. Persia, however, had been the main source of Eastern civilisation, at any rate since the Sassanid period: the debt of Byzantine culture to Persia is well known. Unfortunately no thorough investigation has been made of these various and important changes, but it is clear that Persian civilisation sent its influence far westward, at first directly and later through the medium of Muhammedanism. The same facts hold good with regard to the diffusion of intellectual culture from Persia. How far Persian ideas may have influenced the development of Muhammedan and even of Christian eschatology, we need not here discuss: but the influence of the great Graeco-Christian schools of Persia was enormous: they made the Arabs acquainted with the most important works in Greek and Persian literature. To this fact was due the wide influence of Islam upon Christian civilisation, which is evidenced even to-day by the numerous words of Arab origin to be found in modern

European languages; it is in fact an influence the strength of which can hardly be exaggerated. Not only the commercial products of the East, but important economic methods, the ideals of our so-called European chivalry and of its love poetry, the foundations of our natural sciences, even theological and philosophical ideas of high value were then sent to us from the East. The consequences of the crusades are the best proof of the enormous superiority of the Muhammedan world, a fact which is daily becoming more obvious. Here we are concerned only with the influence exerted by Muhammedan philosophy. It would be more correct to speak of post-classical than of Muhammedan philosophy. But as above, the influence of Christianity upon Islam was considered, so now the reverse process must be outlined. In either case it was the heir to the late classical age, to the mixed Graeco-Oriental culture, which influenced Islam at first in Christian guise. Islam is often able to supplement its borrowings from Christianity at the original sources, and when they have thus been deepened and purified, these adaptations are returned to Christianity in Muhammedan form.

Christian scholasticism was first based upon fragments of Aristotle and chiefly inspired by Neo-Platonism: through the Arabs it became acquainted with almost the whole of Aristotle and also with the special methods by which the Arabs approach the problem of this philosophy. To give any detailed account of this influence would be to write a history of mediaeval philosophy in its relation to ecclesiastical doctrine, a task which I feel to be beyond my powers. I shall therefore confine myself to an abstract of the material points selected from the considerable detail which specialists upon the subject have collected: I consider that Arab influence during the first period is best explained by the new wealth of Greek thought which the Arabs appropriated and transmitted to Europe. These new discoveries were the attainments of Greece in the natural sciences and in logic: they extended the scope of dialectic and stimulated the rise of metaphysical theory: the latter, in combination with ecclesiastical dogma and Greek science, became such a system of thought as that expounded in the Summa of Thomas Aquinas. Philosophy remained the handmaid of religion and Arab influence first served only to complete the ecclesiastical philosophy of life.

Eventually, however, the methods of interpretation and criticism, peculiar to the Arabs when dealing with Aristotle became of no less importance than the subject matter of their inquiries. This form of criticism was developed from the emphasis which Islam had long laid upon the value of wisdom, or recognition of the claims of reason. Muhammedan tradition is full of the praises of wisdom, which it also originally regarded as the basis of religion. Reason, however, gradually became an independent power: orthodoxy did not reject reason when it coincided with tradition, but under the influence of Aristotelianism, especially as developed by Averroës, reason became a power opposed to faith. The essential point of the doctrine was that truth was twofold, according to faith and according to reason. Any one who was subtle enough to recognise both kinds of truth could preserve his orthodoxy: but the theory contained one great danger, which was immediately obvious to the Christian church. The consequent struggle is marked by the constant connection of Arab ideas with the characteristic expressions of Christian feeling; these again are connected with the outset of a new period, when the pioneers of the Renaissance liberate the West from the chains of Greek ecclesiastical classicism, from Oriental metaphysical religion and slowly pave the way for the introduction of Germanic ideals directly derived from true classicism. Not until that period does the West burst the bonds in which Orientalism had confined it.

Christianity and Islam then stand upon an equal footing in respect both of intellectual progress and material wealth. But as the West emerges from the shadow-land of the middle ages the more definite becomes its superiority over the East. Western nations become convinced that the fetters which bind them were forged in the East, and when they have shaken off their chains, they discover their own physical and intellectual power. They go forth and create a new world, in which Orientalism finds but scanty room.

The East, however, cannot break away from the theories of life and mind which grew in it and around it. Even at the present day the Oriental is swathed in mediaevalism. A journalist, for instance, however European his mode of life, will write leaders supported by arguments drawn from tradition and will reason after the manner of the old scholasticism. But a change may well take place. Islam may gradually acquire the spirit as well as the form of modern Europe. Centuries were needed before mediaeval Christianity learned the need for submission to the new spirit. Within Christendom itself, it was non-Christian ideas which created the new movement, but these were completely amalgamated with pre-existing Christianity. Thus, too, a Renaissance is possible in the East, not merely by the importation and imitation of European progress, but primarily by intellectual advancement at home even within the sphere of religion.

Our task is drawing to its close. We have passed in review the interaction of Christianity and Islam, so far as the two religions are concerned. It has also been necessary to refer to the history of the two civilisations, for the reason that the two religions penetrate national life, a feature characteristic both of their nature and of the course of development which they respectively followed. This method of inquiry has enabled us to gain an idea of the rise and progress of Muhammedanism as such.

An attempt to explain the points of contact and resemblance between the two religions naturally tends to obscure the differences between them. Had we devoted our attention to Islam alone, without special reference to Christianity, these differences, especially in the region of dogmatic theology, would have been more obvious. They are, however, generally well known. The points of connection are much more usually disregarded: yet they alone can explain the interchange of thought between the two mediaeval civilisations. The surprising fact is the amount of general similarity in religious theory between religions so fundamentally divergent upon points of dogma. Nor is the similarity confined to religious theory: when we realise that material civilisation, especially when European medievalism was at its height, was practically identical in the Christian West and the Muhammedan East, we are justified in any reference to the unity of Eastern and Western civilisation.

My statements may tend to represent Islam as a religion of no special originality; at the same time, Christianity was but one of other influences operative upon it; early Arabic, Zoroastrian, and Jewish beliefs in particular have left traces on its development. May not as much be said of Christianity? Inquirers have seriously attempted to distinguish Greek and Jewish influences as the component elements of Christianity: in any case, the extent of the elements original to the final orthodox system remains a matter of dispute. As we learn to appreciate historical connection and to probe beneath the surface of religions in course of development, we discover points of relationship and interdependency of which the simple believer never even dreams. The object of all this investigation is, in my opinion, one only: to discover how the religious experience of the founder of a faith accommodates itself to pre-existing civilisation, in the effort to make its influence operative. The eventual triumph of the new religion is in every case and at every time nothing more than a compromise: nor can more be expected, inasmuch as the religious instinct, though one of the most important influences in man, is not the sole determining influence upon his nature.

Recognition of this fact can only be obtained at the price of a breach with ecclesiastical mode of thought. Premonitions of some such breach are apparent in modern Muhammedanism: for ourselves, they are accomplished facts. If I correctly interpret the signs of the times, a retrograde movement in religious development has now begun. The religion inspiring a single personality, has secured domination over the whole of life: family, society, and state have bowed beneath its power. Then the reaction begins: slowly religion loses its comprehensive force and as its history is learned, even at the price of sorrow, it slowly recedes within the true limits of its operation, the individual, the personality, in which it is naturally rooted.

CONCLUSION AND BIBLIOGRAPHY

The purpose of the present work has been to show not so much the identity of Christian and Muhammedan theories of life during the middle ages, as the parallel course of development common to both, and to demonstrate the fact that ideas could be transferred from one system to the other. Detail has been sacrificed to this general purpose. The brief outline of Muhammedan dogmatics and mysticism was necessary to complete the general survey of the question. Any one of these subjects, and the same is true as regards a detailed life of Muhammed, would require at least another volume of equal size for satisfactory treatment.

The Oriental scholar will easily see where I base my statements upon my own researches and where I have followed Goldziher and Snouck. My chief source of information, apart from the six great books of tradition, has been the invaluable compilation of Soj[=u]t[=i], the great Kanz el-'Umm[=a]l (Hyderabad, 1314). To those who do not read Arabic may be recommended the French translation of the Boch[=a]r[=i], of which two volumes are now published: _El-Bokâhri, les traditions islamiques traduites ... par_ O. Houdas and W. Marçais. Paris, 1906.

Of general works dealing with the questions I have touched, the following, to which I owe a considerable debt, may be recommended:--

J. Goldziher. Muhammedanische Studien, Halle, 1889 and following year.

Die Religion des Islams (Kult. d. Gegenw., I, iii. 1).

C. Snouck Hurgronje. De Islam (de Gids, 1886, us. 5 f.). Mekka. The Hague, 1888.

Une nouvelle biographie de Mohammed (Rev. Hist. Relig., 1894).

Leone Caetani di Teano. Annali dell' Islam. Milan, 1905 and following years.

F. Buhl. Muhammed's Liv. Copenhagen, 1903.

H. Grimme. Muhammed. Munich, 1904.

J. Wellhausen. Das arabische Reich und sein Sturz. Berlin, 1902.

Th. Nöldeke. Geschichte des Qoräns. Gottingen, 1860. (New edition by F. Schwally in the press.)

C.H. Becker. Die Kanzel im Kultus des alten Islam. Giessen, 1906.

Papyri. Schott-Reinhardt, I. Heidelberg, 1906.

Th. W. Juynboll. Handleidung tot de kennis van de Mohammedaansche Wet. Leyden, 1903.

T.J. de Boer. Geschichte der Philosophie in Islam. Stuttgart, 1901 (also an English edition).

D.B. Macdonald. Development of Muslim Theology, Jurisprudence and Constitutional Theory. New York, 1903.

A. Merx. Idee und Grundlinien einer allgemeinen Geschichte der Mystik. Heidelberg, 1893.

A. Müller. Der Islam im Morgen- und Abendland (Oncken's collection).

W. Riedel. Die Kirchenrechtsquellen des Patriarchats Alexandrien. Leipsic, 1900.

G. Bruns and E. Sachau. Syrisch-römisches Rechtsbuch. Leipsic, 1880.

E. Sachau. Syrische Rechtsbücher, I. Berlin, 1907.

E. Zachariae v. Lingenthal. Geschichte des griechisch-römischen Rechts. 3rd ed., Berlin, 1892.

H. v. Eicken. Geschichte und System der mittelalterlichen Weltanschauung. Stuttgart, 1886.

W. Windelband. Lehrbuck der Geschichte der Philosophie. 4th ed., Tübingen, 1907.

C. Baeumker und G. v. Hertling. Beiträge zur Geschichte der Philosophie des Mittelalters (collected papers).

G. Gothein. Ignatius von Loyola und die Gegenreformation. Halle, 1895.

In conclusion, I may mention two works, which deal with the subject of this volume, but from a different standpoint:--

H.P. Smith. The Bible and Islam (The Ely Lectures for 1897).

W.A. Shedd. Islam and the Oriental Churches (Philadelphia, 1904).

Made in the USA
Lexington, KY
25 April 2014